1 Noodle — 50 Sauces

Everyday Pasta

> Author: Reinhardt Hess | Photos: Jörn Rynio

Contents

The Fundamentals

The Recipes

Appendices

Everybody Loves Pasta and Sauce

Pasta is always a wonderfully satisfying food for everyone. Children love it and adults adore it, whether tossed simply with butter and cheese or with a more elegant sauce. The best Italian sauce often consists only of butter or extra virgin olive oil and a few, very fine ingredients quickly tossed together. This book provides you with everyday recipes that are sure to succeed plus a few more sophisticated recipes for special occasions. It's the magical "pastasciutta" just like mamma used to make!

Basic Recipe

What you need

One large pot (2 gallon) that allows you to cook your pasta in boiling water without having it stick together. A long-handled, wooden fork (the fork from a set of salad utensils or a wooden spoon works well). A colander, preferably with a rounded bottom, which will allow the water to drain rapidly. Pasta tongs or a pasta rake.

Cooking the Pasta

SERVES 4:

➤ **1 pound pasta**
  4 tbs salt

Sauce in an Instant

Butter and Sage

To serve 4, melt 4 oz butter in a small pan over medium heat. Add 12 sage leaves and sauté for 3–4 minutes until crispy. Pour sage butter over pasta immediately after draining in a colander. Sprinkle with freshly grated parmesan cheese and serve.

> **1** *Bring water to a boil: 1 quart water per 4 oz pasta, plus 1 quart for the pot, (i.e. 5 quarts water for 1 pound pasta).*

> **2** *Wait until the water is boiling to add the salt: No more than 1 tbs per 4 oz pasta. Add pasta immediately after the salt and stir.*

> **3** *Cook pasta according to the directions on the package until "al dente." Just to be sure, test it 1 minute before the specified cooking time has elapsed.*

> **4** *When the pasta is cooked, pour pasta ⌐ water into a colande Let water drain out and immediately tos pasta with the sauce or distribute on plate*

Troubleshooting

It's taking so long for the water to boil!

➤ Make sure you use a pot that lies absolutely flat on the burner when hot. Old, enameled or aluminum pots usually don't. Also, the diameter of the pot should match the diameter of the burner to ensure efficient heating. Cover the pot with the lid until the water boils to save time and energy.

Help! The pasta water is boiling over!

➤ Keep a cup of cold water next to the pot so you can quickly add a bit should the boiling water overflow. Pour in only enough water to stop the foam from rising; you want the pasta water to continue to boil. You can also adjust the heat so that the water only bubbles gently.

Help! The pasta is sticking together!

➤ Did you use too little water (see basic recipe), cover the pot while the pasta was cooking or forget to stir it well from time to time? Pasta must always be cooked in a large amount of water to keep it from sticking. If you don't stir it once in a while, the pasta will stick together regardless of how much water is in the pot. The same thing happens if you drain the pasta and let is sit for too long. The pasta should be kept moist up until the time it is served.

After I cook pasta, the pot is gray!

➤ Always wait until the water is bubbling to add the salt; otherwise, it leaves a gray residue on the pot and the pasta. After pouring out the water, immediately fill the pot with cold water. If necessary, clean the pot with a bit of distilled vinegar to remove the buildup.

The pasta is done but the sauce isn't ready!

➤ You should try to make sure that this does not happen but if it does, take $1/2$ cup of the pasta water before draining and pour it into a large bowl. Then drain the pasta, pour it into the bowl with the water and toss it around. Keep this bowl warm over a double boiler until the sauce is ready.

The sauce is done but the pasta isn't ready!

➤ Pour the sauce into a large bowl and hold in an oven set at its lowest temperature. When the pasta is done, drain it, add to the bowl and quickly toss with the sauce.

Italian Pasta Varieties

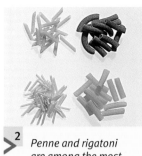

Italian pasta is available in many varieties. It's almost always made of durum wheat semolina and remains al dente (has a slight bite to it) when you cook it. Many types are also available in a variety of colors: Green pasta dyed with spinach, red dyed with tomatoes, beets or chili peppers and black dyed with squid ink.

1 | Long Varieties

Spaghetti is a truly universal pasta variety that goes with all sauces. Bucatini is slightly thicker than spaghetti and hollow. It goes well with hearty, dark sauces containing

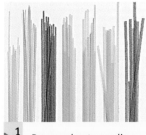

> **1** *Durum wheat semolina or whole-grain spaghetti can be found in almost every household.*

meat and vegetables. Spaghettini and capellini are thinner than spaghetti and are eaten with light sauces and seafood. Bavette and linguine look like spaghetti that's been squashed flat and are served with a fish, seafood or herb sauce. Flat strips or ribbons come in various widths and shapes. Listed from narrowest to widest, they include tagliolini, taglierini, linguine, tagliatelle, fettuccine, pappardelle and reginette (with wavy edges). Rule of thumb: The narrower the pasta, the lighter the sauce. The wider varieties with wavy edges are best with dark, stewed meat sauces.

2 | Short Varieties

Macaroni, available in both short and long varieties, can be used in almost any recipe that calls for short pasta. Penne (pasta tubes with the ends cut on an angle) is extremely versatile. It comes in smooth and ribbed (rigate) varieties and is good at absorbing tomato and meat sauces that are not too thick. The same can be said of the

> **2** *Penne and rigatoni are among the most traditional varieties of short pasta.*

fatter, ribbed tube pasta rigatoni and tortiglioni, as well as matriciani (open tube pasta) and gobbetti (small, crinkled macaroni). Fusilli and spirali (spiral pasta), on the other hand, are ideal for somewhat thicker tomato, vegetable and meat sauces. Farfalle (butterfly pasta) is especially pretty and is an excellent accompaniment to light sauces with cream, ham or salmon.

➤ **Important:** The pasta varieties named in these recipes are only suggestions. You're free to make substitutions based on preference and availability.

Cheese: The Right Partner for Pasta

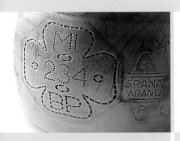

Grana Padano: Hard cheese made from cow's milk with a grainy consistency like Parmesan. Similar to Parmesan, it is shaped into wheels but is aged for a shorter period of time, giving it a milder flavor. **Good for:** Lighter sauces, e.g. with leek and cream or with pumpkin or mushrooms.

Parmigiano Reggiano: The true Parmesan, produced only from April to November and only from cow's milk. It has a spicy, nutty aroma but is never sharp. **Good for:** Tangy sauces, e.g. with ground meat and tomatoes, with ham or chicken livers. **Important:** Buy whole chunks and grate directly over the pasta.

Pecorino: A sheep's cheese from various regions of Italy. Ranges from mild to spicy and sharp, depending on its origin and age. Pecorino Romano (sharp) and Pecorino Toscano (tangy) are the types most often available for grating. **Good for:** Hearty sauces, e.g. with ham, lamb or tomatoes and pepperoncini.

Gorgonzola: Hearty, mild and creamy blue cheese, which is sold in wheels wrapped in silver foil. **Good for:** Fast, tangy sauces, e.g. cream and sage, with nuts or asparagus. **Important:** For cheese sauces, use Gorgonzola that isn't too ripe and spicy.

Mozzarella: Originally made from buffalo milk (mozzarella di bufala), now primarily made from cow's milk. Buffalo mozzarella, soft balls with a slightly sour taste, is tangier than the cow's milk varieties. This cheese melts easily, has little aroma and thickens sauces. **Good for:** Creamy sauces, e.g. with herbs or cherry tomatoes.

Ricotta, Ricotta Salata: Two very different cheeses. Ricotta is a type of creamy, crumbly quark made from cow's milk whereas Ricotta Salata is a more solid, aromatic sheep's cheese that can be grated. **Good for:** Slightly aromatic sauces, e.g. with garlic and mint, with olives or fried eggplant.

7

Basic Recipe

This simple tomato sauce always comes in handy, as a base for both ground meat and vegetable sauces. Or simply toss this sauce with pasta, top with freshly grated or shaved cheese and your "pastasciutta" is ready!

Tomato Sauce

FOR 2 CUPS SAUCE:

- ➤ 2½ pounds ripe tomatoes (preferably plum tomatoes)
- 1 onion
- 1 clove garlic
- 3 sprigs basil
- 3 tbs olive oil
- Salt
- Freshly ground pepper
- 1 pinch sugar

TIP

Stocking up on sauce

When sun-ripened, splendidly aromatic tomatoes are available, prepare twice as much sauce, seal by portions in air-tight containers and freeze. This isn't much more work and you'll have a sauce that's available on short notice and tastes great.

1 Wash tomatoes, remove cores and chop. Peel onions and garlic and chop finely. Remove basil leaves from stems.

2 In a large pot, heat olive oil. Sauté onion and garlic for about 5 minutes over medium heat but don't brown.

3 Add chopped tomatoes with the seeds (important for the flavor) and basil stems and simmer uncovered for 1 hour over low heat until the sauce thickens.

4 Put sauce through a strainer; reduce slight if necessary. Season with salt, pepper and sugar. Finely chop basil leaves and stir into the sauce.

Tomatoes—The Most Important Types

Plum tomatoes:
These are the traditional sauce tomatoes from Italy. They're oblong with a lot of firm meat and few seeds, very aromatic but with a firm peel that can easily be removed after you pour boiling water over them. When purchasing, make sure they're bright red; light-red tomatoes have little aroma. Plum tomatoes are also available canned and are the best substitute for fresh tomatoes in the winter and spring.

Round tomatoes: The most common tomatoes with relatively little meat and lots of seeds that are, however, easy to remove. Only the sun-ripened ones have a tangy sweet aroma; otherwise, their flavor tends to be more bitter and sour. Rule of thumb: The smaller the tomatoes, the tangier they are. Important: For tomato sauces that are put through a strainer, stew the tomatoes with the peels and seeds to augment the aroma.

Beefsteak tomatoes:
These are the largest tomatoes, ribbed and often with a green "collar." They are especially meaty (hence the name) with few seeds, are very juicy and have a sweet, acidic flavor. Important: For sauces, pour boiling water over the tomatoes, peel and cut away green parts. You don't usually need to remove the seeds.

Cherry tomatoes:
Smaller tomatoes, these often come with the green stems attached. Recently, yellow and orange cherry tomatoes have also become available; although decorative, they are generally less aromatic. Red cherry tomatoes are almost always tangier than the larger varieties and can be used unpeeled to make a quick sauce—simply halve or quarter them and heat briefly.

Spicy Oils and Sauces to Keep on Hand

Soffritto

For 2 jars (approx 1 cup each), peel 2 onions, 4 cloves garlic and 2 carrots. Clean, rinse and dry 2 stalks celery, 3 sprigs basil and 3 sprigs parsley. Dice everything finely and mix well with a generous amount of salt. Layer in glasses, adding more salt as you go. Store in a cool, dark place. Suggested use: Briefly heat a little soffritto in olive oil until it gives off an aroma, then add the other ingredients.

Olio Santo

For 1 bottle (2 cups), preheat oven to 400. Rinse 7 pepperoncini (or chile peppers) and remove seeds (or leave the seeds for a spicier oil). Place peppers on a baking sheet and roast in the oven (center rack) for 6–7 minutes until slightly brown. Transfer to a bottle and pour in 2 cups extra virgin olive oil. Marinate 2 weeks in a dark place. Suggested use: Season sauces to taste with a few drops of olio santo or place the bottle on the table to be used for seasoning.

Herb Oil

For 1 bottle (2 cups), place 2 sprigs rosemary, 2 sprigs thyme, 2 sprigs oregano and 2 bay leaves in the bottle. Peel 2 cloves garlic, crush them slightly with a knife and add them to the herbs. Pour in 2 cups extra virgin olive oil. Marinate at least 2–3 weeks in a cool dark place (but not in the refrigerator). Suggested use: Stir a little (or more) oil into the pasta.

Spicy Mushrooms

For 1 jar (1½ cups), peel and mince 1 onion and 2 cloves garlic. Finely chop leaves from ½ bunch parsley, 1 sprig rosemary, 2 sprigs oregano and 2 sprigs basil. Saute all these ingredients in 3 tbs olive oil for 3 minutes. Dice 7 oz mushrooms very finely, add to oil and sauté for 5 minutes. Season with salt and pepper. Transfer to the jar and pour in ½ cup extra virgin olive oil. Store in a cool, dark place. Suggested use: Stir a little bit of the mushrooms into drained pasta along with a little pasta water.

esto alla Genovese

or 1 jar (1 cup), remove
aves from 2 bunches
asil. Peel and coarsely
hop 3 cloves garlic.
inely crush both in a
ortar or in a blender
long with 1 oz pine
uts and a little sea
alt. Add 1 oz each of
eshly grated Pecorino
nd Parmesan and
radually mix in about
2 cup extra virgin olive
il until you have a
reamy sauce. Pour
nto the jar and store
a cool, dark place.
uggested use: Mix
esto with drained
asta.

Pesto Rosso

For 1 jar (1 cup), coarsely
chop 6 oz sun-dried
tomatoes in oil and 2 oz
pitted black olives. Purée
while adding 1/4 cup
extra virgin olive oil.
Stir in 1 crushed, dried
pepperoncino and 1/2
tsp dried oregano. Peel
3 cloves garlic, squeeze
through a press and
add. Stew every-thing
for 5–10 minutes over
low heat and season with
salt. Transfer to the jar
and store in a cool, dark
place. Suggested use:
Stir into drained pasta
along with a little
pasta water.

Bomba Vulcanica

For 1 jar (1 cup), rinse
6 oz pepperoncini (or
chile pepper), remove
stems and seeds and
chop finely. Braise in
1/2 cup extra virgin olive
oil for 10–15 minutes
over low heat until ten-
der. Peel 2 cloves garlic,
squeeze through a press
and add. Season with
3 tbs white wine vinegar,
1 pinch dried thyme,
1 pinch dried oregano,
salt and pepper. Transfer
to the jar and store in a
cool dark place (but not
the refrigerator).
Suggested use: Stir into
pasta either by itself or
with a little pasta water.

Walnut Sauce

For 1 jar (1 cup), remove
leaves from 3 sprigs
basil. Toast 2 tbs pine
nuts without oil until
golden brown. Peel and
coarsely chop 3 cloves
garlic. Purée all these
ingredients with 5 oz
walnuts while gradually
adding 1/2 cup extra
virgin olive oil to form
a creamy sauce. Season
to taste with salt and
pepper. Transfer to
jar and store in a cool,
dark place. Suggested
use: Stir into drained
pasta along with a little
pasta water.

Pasta with Cold Sauce

In Italy, these dishes are especially popular in the summer when fast, cold sauces are simply tossed with hot pasta. It's important to remove the pasta from the water and drain it quickly so that it's very hot when the sauce is added. It doesn't hurt anything if the pasta still contains a little water, it just means the sauce will be a little thinner. Be sure to take this into account when adding spices and always season the sauces generously.

Quick Recipes

Farfalle with Herb Butter

SERVES 4:

> ➤ 1 pound farfalle | Salt |
> 4 oz softened herb butter |
> 1 lemon | Freshly ground pepper |
> 3 oz freshly grated Parmesan

1 | Cook pasta according to the basic recipe. In the meantime, stir butter until foamy. Rinse lemon, grate off about 1 tsp zest and squeeze out juice. Stir zest and juice into butter and season to taste with salt and pepper.

2 | Add approx ⅓ cup pasta water to herb butter. Drain pasta briefly and toss with butter. Serve sprinkled with cheese.

Pasta with Pesto and Ham

SERVES 4:

> ➤ 1 pound tagliolini (or fettucine) |
> Salt | 4 oz pesto (see page 11) |
> 2 oz freshly grated Parmesan |
> 4 oz thinly sliced Parma or
> San Daniele ham

1 | Cook pasta according to the basic recipe. Stir together pasta and approx. ⅓ cup pasta water. Drain pasta briefly and immediately toss with pesto.

2 | Distribute pasta on plates, sprinkle with Parmesan, top with ham and serve immediately.

13

Fast | Vegetarian

Pasta with Lemon Sauce

SERVES 4:

➤ 1 pound tagliolini
  (or fettucine)
  Salt
  1 large lemon
  1 clove garlic
  Freshly ground pepper
  1/2 cup olive oil
  2 tbs coarsely
  chopped parsley
  2 oz freshly grated
  Parmesan

🕐 Prep time: 20 minutes
➤ Calories per serving: 610

1 | Cook pasta according to the basic recipe. In the meantime, rinse lemon under hot water and grate off zest. Squeeze out juice and pour through a strainer into a bowl.

2 | Peel garlic, squeeze through a press and add to the bowl. Season with salt and pepper. Beat vigorously with a wire whisk while gradually adding olive oil. Stir in lemon zest and parsley.

3 | Drain pasta briefly and toss immediately with sauce. Serve sprinkled with cheese.

➤ Serve with: Dry,
  delicate white wine

Spicy | Vegetarian

Macaroni with Mascarpone

SERVES 4:

➤ 1 pound macaroni
  Salt
  1 red pepperoncini
  (or chile pepper)
  1 bunch basil
  9 oz Mascarpone (may
  substitute full-fat quark)
  Freshly ground pepper
  Freshly grated nutmeg
  2 oz freshly grated
  Parmesan

🕐 Prep time: 15 minutes
➤ Calories per serving: 730

1 | Cook pasta according to the basic recipe. In the meantime, rinse pepperoncini, slit open lengthwise, remove seeds and stem and cut into very narrow strips. Finely chop basil leaves.

2 | Stir together Mascarpone, pepperoncini and basil until nice and creamy; if necessary, add a little pasta water. Season to taste with salt, pepper and nutmeg.

3 | Drain pasta briefly and toss with Mascarpone cream. Sprinkle with cheese and serve immediately.

➤ Serve with: Aromatic,
  fruity white wine

TIP
To make the Mascarpone Macaroni more colorful, sprinkle the pasta with a few black olives cut into strips along with the cheese.

Photo top: **Pasta with Lemon Sauce**   *Photo bottom:* **Macaroni with Mascarpone** ➤

Impressive | Fast

Macaroni with Asparagus and Tomatoes

SERVES 4:
- ➤ 1 pound green asparagus
  10 oz cherry tomatoes
  1 tbs lemon juice
  Salt
  Freshly ground pepper
  4 tbs olive oil
  1 sprig oregano
  1 pound macaroni
  2 tbs herb butter
  2 oz freshly grated Parmesan

🕐 Prep time: 20 minutes
➤ Calories per serving: 550

1 | Rinse asparagus and cut off ends (for thicker spears, peel lower third and halve spear lengthwise). Cut on an angle into slices about 1 inch long. Rinse and quarter tomatoes.

2 | In a bowl, mix asparagus and tomatoes with lemon juice, salt, pepper and olive oil. Rinse oregano, shake dry and remove leaves.

3 | Cook pasta according to the basic recipe. Drain and toss with herb butter, asparagus and tomatoes. Sprinkle with cheese.

➤ Serve with: Hearty, spicy white wine

Fresh and cold

Pinzimonio Rigatoni

SERVES 4:
- ➤ 1 clove garlic
  6 tbs olive oil
  4 tbs lemon juice
  Several dashes of Tabasco
  Salt
  Freshly ground pepper
  4 scallions
  2 small zucchini
  1 red bell pepper
  1 stalk celery
  $\frac{1}{2}$ head of radicchio
  1 pound rigatoni
  2 oz freshly grated Pecorino

🕐 Prep time: 35 minutes
➤ Calories per serving: 580

1 | Peel garlic and squeeze through a press. Stir together with oil, lemon juice, Tabasco, salt and pepper to form a marinade.

2 | Rinse scallions, clean and dice white part. Slice green part into fine rings and set aside. Rinse zucchini, clean and dice finely. Rinse bell pepper, cut in half, clean and dice finely. Rinse celery and cut into thin slices. Rinse radicchio, quarter and cut into narrow strips. Mix all vegetables (except scallion greens) with the marinade.

3 | Cook pasta according to the basic recipe. Drain briefly and toss immediately with the pinzimonio sauce. Distribute on plates and sprinkle with scallion greens and Pecorino.

➤ Serve with: Spicy, fruity white wine

Vegetarian | Fast
Tortiglioni "Tricolori"

SERVES 4:
- ➤ 1 pound tortiglioni (or penne)
  Salt
  12 oz cherry tomatoes
  2 balls Mozzarella (8 oz)
  2 cloves garlic
  1 bunch basil
  4 tbs olive oil
  Freshly ground pepper
  Pinch cayenne pepper

🕐 Prep time: 20 minutes
➤ Calories per serving: 610

1 | Cook pasta according to the basic recipe. In the meantime, rinse tomatoes and cut in half. Cut Mozzarella into cubes of about ½ inch. Peel garlic cloves, cut in half and rub one half on the inside of a metal bowl. Remove basil leaves from stems.

2 | Drain pasta briefly and pour into the bowl. Toss with tomatoes, Mozzarella, basil and olive oil. Season with salt and a lot of pepper.

Add cayenne and serve immediately.

➤ Serve with: Fruity red wine

Specialty of Rome
Linguine with Ricotta and Mint

SERVES 4:
- ➤ 1 pound green linguine
  Salt
  8 oz Ricotta Salata
  3 sprigs mint (may substitute basil)
  2 cloves garlic
  2 oz butter
  2 tsp coarsely ground pepper

🕐 Prep time: 20 minutes
➤ Calories per serving: 545

1 | Cook pasta according to the basic recipe. Crumble Ricotta with your fingers. Rinse mint, shake dry and set several leaves aside for garnish. Cut remaining leaves into narrow strips or chop coarsely.

2 | Peel garlic cloves, cut in half and rub one half on the inside of a large bowl. Cut butter into bits, place in the bowl along with 4–6 tbs pasta water and stir vigorously.

3 | Drain pasta briefly and transfer to the bowl. Toss with butter, a little salt, pepper, chopped mint and ricotta. Distribute on plates, garnish with whole mint leaves and serve immediately.

➤ Serve with: Hearty, fruity white wine

TIP
The Linguine also tastes excellent if you leave out the Ricotta Salata and instead grate mild Pecorino Romano over the pasta. Or give the pasta a spicy accent by substituting a large shot of olio santo (see page 10) for the cheese.

Fast | Easy

Spaghetti with Shrimp and Raisins

SERVES 4:

➤ **2 tbs raisins**
3 tbs brandy
3 tbs orange liqueur (may substitute orange juice)
1 pound spaghetti
Salt
3–4 leaves romaine lettuce
10 oz cooked, peeled shrimp
2 tbs lemon juice
6 tbs olive oil
Freshly ground pepper

⏲ Prep time: 25 minutes
➤ Calories per serving: 620

1 | Soak raisins in brandy and orange liqueur. Cook pasta according to the basic recipe.

2 | Rinse lettuce leaves, spin dry and cut into narrow strips. Combine shrimp, raisins, brandy, liqueur, lemon juice and olive oil. Season to taste with salt and pepper.

3 | Drain pasta briefly and toss with the shrimp sauce and a little pasta water. Stir in lettuce and serve immediately.

➤ Serve with:
Fresh white wine

Specialty of Liguria

Linguine with Arugula Walnut Pesto

SERVES 4:

➤ **5 oz arugula**
2 oz walnuts
1 clove garlic
1 pound linguine
Salt
Coarse sea salt
1/3 cup olive oil
Freshly ground pepper
3 oz freshly grated Parmesan

⏲ Prep time: 25 minutes
➤ Calories per serving: 675

1 | Sort arugula and remove hard stems. Rinse leaves, spin dry and chop coarsely. Break walnuts into small pieces. Peel garlic and chop coarsely. Cook pasta according to the basic recipe.

2 | Crush arugula, walnuts, garlic and sea salt in a mortar or purée finely in a blender while gradually adding oil. When the pesto becomes creamy, season to taste with salt and pepper.

3 | Add about 4 tbs pasta water to the pesto. Drain pasta briefly and toss immediately with pesto. Transfer to plates and serve sprinkled with cheese.

➤ Serve with: Smooth, fruity white wine

TIP The pesto will have even more flavor if you toast the walnuts in a small pan without oil before breaking them up.

Photo top: **Spaghetti with Shrimp and Raisins**   *Photo bottom:* **Linguine with Arugula Walnut Pesto** ➤

Inexpensive | Tangy

Pasta with Raw Tomatoes

SERVES 4:

- ➤ 1 bunch basil
  4 tbs olive oil
  1 pound macaroni
  Salt
  2¼ pounds ripe tomatoes
  2 cloves garlic
  Freshly ground pepper
  1 pinch cayenne pepper (may substitute 1 tbs olio santo, see page 10)

- ⏱ Prep time: 30 minutes
- ➤ Calories per serving: 490

1 | Cut basil leaves into narrow strips and stir into olive oil.

2 | Cook pasta according to the basic recipe. Remove cores from tomatoes, pour boiling water over the top, peel, cut in half and remove seeds. Dice finely and add to basil. Peel garlic, squeeze through a press and add. Season with salt, pepper and cayenne.

3 | Drain pasta briefly and toss with tomato sauce. Serve immediately.

- ➤ Serve with: Smooth, mild red wine

Traditional Dish with a New Twist

Taglierini with Salmon Cream

SERVES 4:

- ➤ 2 slices sandwich bread
  2 tbs white wine vinegar
  6 oz sliced smoked salmon
  2 cloves garlic
  ¼ cup olive oil
  3 tbs white wine (may substitute vegetable stock)
  1 tbs capers
  1 pound taglierini (or linguine)
  Salt
  Freshly ground pepper
  1 bunch watercress

- ⏱ Prep time: 30 minutes
- ➤ Calories per serving: 655

1 | Remove crust from bread, sprinkle bread with vinegar and 1–2 tbs water and let soak. Cut 2 slices smoked salmon into narrow strips, cover and refrigerate. Coarsely chop remaining salmon. Place in a blender along with bread.

2 | Peel garlic, squeeze through a press and add. Purée with salmon and bread while gradually adding olive oil. Stir in enough white wine to make the sauce nice and creamy. Add capers and blend briefly. Season to taste with salt and pepper.

3 | Cook pasta according to the basic recipe. Rinse watercress, snip off leaves with scissors and sprinkle over salmon cream.

4 | Drain pasta briefly and toss with salmon cream and watercress. Serve garnished with salmon strips.

- ➤ Serve with: Fruity rosé

Pasta with Vegetables, Mushrooms and Nuts

Crisp, fresh vegetables or mushrooms and nuts often play a much greater role in Italian pasta sauces than meat or seafood. More and more, people are choosing more economical "sauces" made with ingredients culled from farms and gardens—in other words, "simple pasta sauces" that demonstrate the extreme versatility of Italian cuisine.

Quick Recipes

Tagliatelle with Oyster Mushrooms

SERVES 4:

➤ 10 oz oyster mushrooms | 2 scallions |
2 cloves garlic | 1 pound green
tagliatelle | Salt | 2 tbs olive oil |
2 tbs butter | Freshly ground pepper

1 | Clean mushrooms, remove ends of
stems and cut caps into wide strips. Rinse
scallions, clean and chop into fine rings.
Peel garlic and mince.

2 | Cook pasta according to the basic recipe.
In the meantime, heat oil and butter and
sauté mushrooms, onions and garlic for
5 minutes over medium heat. Season with
salt and pepper. Drain pasta, transfer to
plates and top with mushrooms.

Spirali with Pine Nuts and Sage

SERVES 4:

➤ 1 pound spirali | Salt | 2 sprigs sage |
3 oz butter | 2 oz pine nuts |
Freshly ground pepper | 2 oz freshly
grated Parmesan

1 | Cook pasta according to the basic
recipe. In the meantime, rinse sage, shake
dry and remove leaves. Melt butter, add
sage leaves and pine nuts and let foam up
briefly over medium heat. Pour in 1/4 cup
pasta water and season to taste with salt.

2 | Drain pasta, transfer to plates and top
with sage pine-nut butter. Serve sprinkled
with pepper and cheese.

Traditional | Spicy

Bucatini Abruzzo Style

SERVES 4:

- ➤ 1 pound bucatini
  Salt
  1¼ pounds broccoli
  4 cloves garlic
  4 anchovy fillets in brine
  4 tbs olive oil
  1 tsp small, dried pepper-oncini (or chile pepper)
  Freshly ground pepper

- ⏱ Prep time: 20 minutes
- ➤ Calories per serving: 480

1 | Cook pasta according to the basic recipe. Rinse broccoli, clean and divide into small florets. Depending on the size, cut stem into quarters or eighths. When the pasta has cooked for 5 minutes, add broccoli and cook for remaining time.

2 | Peel garlic and slice. Rinse anchovies and chop. Heat 1 tbs oil. Crumble pepperoncini into oil, stir in garlic and sauté briefly for 3–4 minutes over low heat until translucent. Add anchovies and stir briefly.

3 | Remove pasta and broccoli from water, drain and immediately toss with garlic anchovy oil and remaining olive oil. Season with salt and pepper and serve immediately.

- ➤ Serve with:
  Fruity white wine

Original | Sophisticated

Taglierini with Swiss Chard

SERVES 4:

- ➤ 1½ pounds Swiss chard, baby leaves are preferable
  Salt
  4 oz cooked ham (without fat or rind)
  1 large onion
  4 tbs olive oil
  2 oz black olives
  6 oz vegetable stock
  1 pound taglierini (or linguine)
  Freshly ground pepper
  2 oz whole Parmesan piece

- ⏱ Prep time: 45 minutes
- ➤ Calories per serving: 585

1 | Rinse chard, clean and cut stems and leaves into narrow strips. Bring a large amount of water to a boil and add salt. First blanch stems for 3 minutes, then add leaves and cook another 2 minutes. Remove with a slotted spoon and rinse under cold water.

2 | Dice ham finely. Peel onion and mince. Heat oil and sauté onion 5 minutes over medium heat until golden. Add chard, ham and olives. Pour in stock, cover and braise 10 minutes over low heat.

3 | Cook pasta in chard water according to the basic recipe. Drain, toss with sauce and season with salt and pepper. Transfer to plates and shave Parmesan over the top using a vegetable or cheese slicer.

- ➤ Serve with: Dry, not-too-acidic white wine

Photo top: **Bucatini Abruzzo Style**   *Photo bottom:* **Taglierini with Swiss Chard** ➤

Easy | Fruity

Spaghetti with Baked Tomatoes

SERVES 4:

➤ 1¼ pounds small tomatoes
  Salt
  Freshly ground pepper
  2 cloves garlic
  6 tbs olive oil
  1 pound spaghetti
  4 oz arugula
  2 oz whole Pecorino

🕐 Prep time: 35 minutes
➤ Calories per serving: 570

1 | Preheat oven to 400°F. Rinse tomatoes, cut in half and remove cores. Place on a baking dish with the cut sides up and season lightly with salt and pepper. Peel garlic and squeeze through a press. Combine garlic with 2 tbs oil and brush onto tomatoes. Bake in oven (center rack) for 10 minutes.

2 | Cook pasta according to the basic recipe. In the meantime, sort arugula and remove hard stems. Rinse leaves, spin dry and chop coarsely.

3 | Drain pasta briefly and toss with remaining oil, baked tomatoes and arugula. Transfer to plates and shave Pecorino over the top using a vegetable or cheese slicer.

➤ Serve with: Semi-fruity red wine

Specialty of Ischia

Bavette "Donna di Strada"

SERVES 4:

➤ 2 tbs small capers (preferably in brine)
  4 anchovies in brine
  4 cloves garlic
  2 oz black olives
  12 oz cherry tomatoes
  1 pound bavette (or linguine)
  Salt
  4 tbs olive oil
  4 tbs chopped parsley
  Cayenne pepper

🕐 Prep time: 30 minutes
➤ Calories per serving: 490

1 | Rinse capers and anchovies. Finely chop anchovies. Peel garlic and chop coarsely.

Remove pits from olives and cut into strips. Rinse cherry tomatoes and cut in half.

2 | Cook pasta according to the basic recipe. Heat oil and briefly sauté garlic over low heat until translucent. Add tomatoes, capers and olives, pour in about ½ cup of pasta water and simmer gently for 5 minutes.

3 | Stir anchovies into sauce until they disintegrate. Add parsley and season sauce with a little salt and a lot of cayenne. Remove from heat.

4 | Drain pasta briefly and toss with the sauce.

➤ Serve with: Fresh, fruity, light, almost mild white wine

Sophisticated | Fast

Farfalle with Two Types of Peas

SERVES 4:

- ➤ 1 pound farfalle
  Salt
  5 oz snow peas
  2 oz sliced prosciutto
  4 oz mushrooms
  1 tbs butter
  1 tbs olive oil
  3 oz frozen peas
  1 cup cream
  Freshly ground pepper
  Freshly grated nutmeg
  2 oz freshly grated Parmesan

- ⏱ Prep time: 20 minutes
- ➤ Calories per serving: 730

1 | Cook pasta according to the basic recipe. Rinse snow peas and cut into narrow strips. Remove fat from prosciutto. Dice fat finely and cut meat into strips. Clean mushrooms and slice.

2 | Heat butter and oil and render diced fat for 4–5 minutes over low heat. Add prosciutto strips, snow peas, mushrooms and frozen peas and cook for 5 minutes.

3 | Add cream to vegetables. Season with salt, pepper and nutmeg and simmer for another 5 minutes.

4 | Drain pasta briefly and toss with the sauce. Serve sprinkled with cheese.

- ➤ Serve with: Fruity white

Original | Sophisticated

Rigatoni with Pumpkin Mousse

SERVES 4:

- ➤ 10 oz pumpkin flesh
  3 oz butter
  Salt
  1 pound rigatoni
  1½ oz. amaretti (almond cookies)
  ¼ cup cream
  Freshly ground pepper
  Freshly grated nutmeg
  2 oz freshly grated Grana Padano

- ⏱ Prep time: 35 minutes
- ➤ Calories per serving: 715

1 | Chop pumpkin coarsely. Melt 1 tbs butter and braise pumpkin for 1–2 minutes. Add just enough water to barely cover pumpkin, season with salt, cover and braise for about 20 minutes over low heat until tender. Cook pasta according to the basic recipe.

2 | Place amaretti in a plastic bag and crush with a rolling pin. Using a hand or electric blender, purée pumpkin until smooth while gradually adding 2 tbs butter and cream. Season with salt, pepper and nutmeg.

3 | Heat remaining butter, add amaretti and let foam up. Drain pasta briefly and toss with pumpkin sauce. Transfer to plates, pour amaretti butter over the top and serve sprinkled with cheese.

- ➤ Serve with: Smooth white wine

Fast | For Company

Fusilli "Trifolati"

SERVES 4:

- 1¼ pounds crimini (brown) mushrooms
  1 bunch scallions
  2 cloves garlic
  1 pound fusilli
  Salt
  4 tbs olive oil
  ⅔ cup white wine (may substitute vegetable stock)
  Freshly ground pepper
  1 pinch cayenne pepper
  2 tbs chopped parsley
  2 oz freshly grated Parmesan

- Prep time: 25 minutes
- Calories per serving: 555

1 | Clean mushrooms and cut into thin slices. Rinse onions, clean and cut into thin rings. Peel garlic and mince.

2 | Cook pasta according to the basic recipe. In the meantime, heat olive oil and sauté mushrooms 7 minutes over high heat until all the moisture has been cooked away and they are slightly brown. Switch to medium heat, add garlic and sauté briefly. Pour in wine and season with salt, pepper and cayenne to make it spicy. When almost all the wine has evaporated, stir in parsley and scallions.

3 | Drain pasta, toss with mushrooms and sprinkle with cheese. Serve immediately.

- Serve with: Fruity white wine

Traditional | Fast

Woodcutter's Spaghetti

SERVES 4:

- 10 oz fresh wild mushrooms (may substitute ½ oz dried mushrooms, soaked and squeezed out)
  1½ pounds tomatoes
  1 onion
  5 cloves garlic
  3 tbs olive oil
  1 pound spaghetti
  Salt
  Freshly ground pepper
  1 can tuna in water (6 oz)

- Prep time: 25 minutes
- Cooking time: 15 minutes
- Calories per serving: 520

1 | Clean mushrooms and chop finely. Remove cores from tomatoes, pour boiling water over them, peel and dice finely. Peel onion and garlic and mince.

2 | Heat oil and sauté mushrooms over high heat until the liquid has evaporated. Add onion and garlic and sauté 5 minutes over low heat. Stir in tomatoes and gently simmer uncovered for 15 minutes.

3 | Cook pasta according to the basic recipe. Season sauce with salt and pepper. Stir in tuna along with the water it's packed in, crumbling slightly. Drain pasta and transfer to plates. Top with mushroom sauce.

- Serve with: Dry, fruity rosé

Photo left: **Fusilli "Trifolati"**   *Photo right:* **Woodcutter's Spaghetti**

Specialty of Venice

Spaghetti with Radicchio

SERVES 4:

- ➤ 1 pound spaghetti
  Salt
  2 heads radicchio (preferably radicchio di Treviso, 12 oz)
  3 cloves garlic
  6 tbs olive oil
  2 oz pine nuts
  3 oz freshly shaved Pecorino
  Freshly ground pepper

- ⏱ Prep time: 25 minutes
- ➤ Calories per serving: 690

1 | Cook pasta according to the basic recipe. Clean radicchio, remove leaves, rinse, spin dry and chop finely. Peel garlic and mince. Heat oil in a large pan and sauté garlic and pine nuts over medium heat until light brown.

2 | Drain pasta briefly. Add to pan along with half the radicchio and heat while stirring. Stir in half the cheese and season with salt and pepper. Serve sprinkled with remaining Pecorino and radicchio.

- ➤ Serve with: Fruity white wine from Sardinia

Fast | Vegetarian

Gobbetti with Orange Gremolata

SERVES 4:

- ➤ 1 oz pine nuts
  1 oz walnuts
  Finely chopped zest from 1 orange
  2 tbs chopped parsley
  1 tsp chopped rosemary
  2 tbs olive oil
  3 cloves garlic
  1 pound gobbetti (or macaroni)
  Salt
  1 cup cream
  4 oz Gorgonzola
  Freshly ground pepper
  Freshly grated nutmeg
  2 oz freshly grated Parmesan

- ⏱ Prep time: 30 minutes
- ➤ Calories per serving: 915

1 | Coarsely chop pine nuts and walnuts and toast briefly over low heat in a small pan without oil. Stir in orange zest, parsley, rosemary and oil. Peel garlic, squeeze through a press and add to pan.

2 | Cook pasta according to the basic recipe. Heat orange nut mixture over low heat until the oil sizzles slightly. Pour in cream and simmer gently for about 5 minutes.

3 | Mash Gorgonzola with a fork, stir into sauce and let melt. Season sauce with salt, pepper and nutmeg.

4 | Drain pasta briefly and toss with orange gremolata. Serve sprinkled with Parmesan.

- ➤ Serve with: Dry, smooth white wine

TIP

To get the most flavor from orange peels, use only the colored part (zest) and not the white.

Pasta with Fish and Seafood

Like many places, fish and seafood have become expensive in Italy so they're being used more and more in pasta sauces where a small amount suffices to bring the "sea" to your plate. Commercial fish like salmon are often used, which are not local to the Mediterranean but available fresh and inexpensive. But Italian favorites continue to be scampi, small lobster and clams.

Quick Recipes

Linguine with Salmon

SERVES 4:

➤ 1 pound linguine │ Salt │
  9 oz salmon fillet │ 1 tsp lemon juice │
  2 cups heavy cream │ 2 tsp lemon pepper │
  2 tbs freshly chopped parsley

1 │ Cook pasta according to the basic recipe.
In the meantime, cut salmon fillet into slices
about ½ inch thick and sprinkle with lemon
juice. Heat cream over low heat and season
with salt and lemon pepper. Stir in salmon
and poach 5 minutes until done.

2 │ Drain pasta briefly. Pour salmon and
sauce over pasta. Serve sprinkled with
parsley— but without cheese!

Spaghettini with Anchovies

SERVES 4:

➤ 1 pound spaghettini (or thin spaghetti) │
  Salt │ 6 anchovy fillets in brine │
  6 tbs olive oil │ 4 cloves garlic │
  2 tbs chopped parsley

1 │ Cook pasta according to the basic recipe.
In the meantime, wipe anchovy fillets with
paper towels and chop finely. Heat oil and
anchovies slowly over low heat. Peel garlic,
squeeze through a press, add and sauté
all these ingredients for 4–5 minutes while
stirring constantly until the anchovies
disintegrate. Pour in no more than ⅓ cup
pasta water and bring to a boil.

2 │ Drain pasta briefly, toss with anchovy
sauce and serve sprinkled with parsley.

Easy | Tangy

Farfalle with Tuna

SERVES 4:

➤ 3 shallots

1 clove garlic

2 tbs olive oil

1/3 cup white wine (may substitute vegetable stock)

3/4 cup vegetable stock

12 oz farfalle

Salt

1/2 cup cream

1 can tuna packed in water (6 oz)

2 tbs small capers

Freshly ground pepper

1 tbs oregano leaves

🕐 Prep time: 25 minutes

➤ Calories per serving: 575

1 | Peel shallots and garlic and mince. Heat oil and sauté both ingredients 3–4 minutes over medium heat until translucent. Pour in wine and reduce almost completely. Pour in stock and simmer for 5 minutes.

2 | Cook pasta according to the basic recipe. Stir cream into sauce and heat. Drain tuna, pull apart with a fork and add to sauce along with capers. Simmer for 5 minutes over medium heat. Season with salt and pepper.

3 | Drain pasta and toss with sauce. Serve sprinkled with oregano.

➤ Serve with: Not-too-acidic white wine

Fast | For Company

Linguine with Salmon and Mint

SERVES 4:

➤ 2 shallots

2 tbs butter

1 tsp grated lemon zest

2/3 cup white wine (may substitute vegetable stock)

1 cup cream

1 pound linguine

Salt

9 oz salmon fillet

Freshly ground pepper

2 tbs lemon liqueur (may substitute lemon juice)

4 sprigs mint

🕐 Prep time: 30 minutes

➤ Calories per serving: 730

1 | Peel shallots and mince. Heat butter over medium heat until foamy and sauté shallots 3–4 minutes until translucent. Add lemon zest and wine and reduce by one third over high heat. Stir in cream and simmer gently over low heat, uncovered, for 10 minutes.

2 | Cook pasta according to the basic recipe. In the meantime, cut salmon into thin slices and stir into cream sauce. Season with salt, pepper and lemon liqueur and poach 2–3 minutes over low heat. Rinse mint, shake dry and coarsely chop leaves.

3 | Drain pasta and toss with sauce. Serve sprinkled with mint.

➤ Serve with: Hearty white wine

Photo top: **Farfalle with Tuna**   *Photo bottom:* **Linguine with Salmon and Mint** ➤

For Gourmets

Bavette Vongole

SERVES 4:

➤ 2¼ pounds
  Cherrystone clams
  2 shallots
  2 cloves garlic
  10 oz zucchini
  1 pound bavette
  (or linguine)
  Salt
  6 tbs olive oil
  Freshly ground pepper
  2 tbs chopped parsley

🕐 Prep time: 40 minutes
➤ Calories per serving: 660

1 | Rinse clams under running water. Throw away any that are damaged or open.

2 | Peel shallots and garlic and mince. Rinse zucchini, clean, cut lengthwise into thin slices and cut slices into very narrow strips. Cook pasta according to the basic recipe.

3 | Heat oil and briefly sauté shallots and garlic 2–3 minutes over low heat. Switch to high heat, add clams, cover and cook for about 5 minutes

until the clams open (throw away any clams that are still closed).

4 | Add zucchini strips and about 1/2 cup pasta water to clams and cook down briefly. Season with salt and pepper. Drain pasta and toss with clam sauce and parsley.

➤ Serve with:
  Fresh white wine

Inexpensive | Easy

Fusilli with Squid Ragout

SERVES 4:

➤ 1 pound squid
  Salt
  3 shallots
  4 cloves garlic
  2 tbs olive oil
  ¾ cup fish stock
  ⅓ cup white wine (may substitute fish stock)
  Freshly ground pepper
  1 pinch cayenne pepper
  1 pound fusilli
  1 tsp lemon juice
  2 tbs chopped parsley

🕐 Prep time: 35 minutes
➤ Calories per serving: 615

1 | Blanch squid for 1 minute in boiling, salted water, pour into a colander and rinse under cold water. Drain and cut into strips.

2 | Peel shallots and garlic and mince. Heat oil and briefly sauté both over medium heat. Pour in stock and wine and reduce for 5 minutes over high heat. Season with salt, pepper and cayenne. Add squid and poach 15 minutes over low heat.

3 | Cook pasta according to the basic recipe. Season squid ragout to taste with lemon juice, salt, pepper and parsley. Drain pasta briefly and toss with ragout.

➤ Serve with:
  Fruity white wine

Photo top: **Bavette Vongole**   *Photo bottom:* **Fusilli with Squid Ragout** ➤

For Gourmets | Fast
Linguine with Lemon Scampi

SERVES 4:

- ➤ 1 large lemon
  4 cloves garlic
  1 pound linguine
  Salt
  4 tbs olive oil
  12 raw shrimp (12 oz, peeled or unpeeled)
  2 tbs Italian brandy (optional)
  2 tbs chopped parsley
  Freshly ground pepper

🕐 Prep time: 20 minutes
➤ Calories per serving: 545

1 | Rinse lemon, grate off about 2 tsp zest and squeeze out juice. Peel garlic. Cook pasta according to the basic recipe.

1 | Heat oil. Add shrimp and stir for 2–3 minutes over medium heat. Squeeze garlic through a press and add to shrimp. Drizzle with brandy. Add parsley, lemon juice and lemon zest and heat but don't boil. Season with salt and pepper.

3 | Drain pasta and transfer to plates. Top with scampi.

➤ Serve with: Decently dry white wine

Specialty of Sicily
Bucatini with Sardines

SERVES 4:

- ➤ 2 oz raisins
  9 oz sardine fillets
  2 cloves garlic
  1 onion
  2 anchovy fillets in brine
  5 tender stalks from a fennel bulb
  4 tbs olive oil
  5 tbs breadcrumbs
  Salt
  1 pound bucatini, broken into pieces
  1 oz pine nuts
  Freshly ground pepper
  1 pinch saffron

🕐 Prep time: 35 minutes
➤ Calories per serving: 665

1 | Barely cover raisins with warm water. Cut sardines into bite-sized pieces. Peel garlic and onion and mince. Rinse anchovy fillets, pat dry and chop finely. Rinse fennel stalks and chop finely. Heat 1 tbs oil and toast breadcrumbs over medium heat until light brown. Set aside.

2 | Bring to a boil enough water to cook the pasta, add salt and blanch fennel for 2–3 minutes. Remove fennel and cook pasta according to the basic recipe. Heat remaining oil and briefly sauté onion and garlic over low to medium heat. Add pine nuts and anchovies and sauté briefly. Add fennel and sardines and braise 4–5 minutes. Stir in raisins with the water. Season with salt, pepper and saffron.

3 | Drain pasta and toss with the sauce. Serve sprinkled with toasted breadcrumbs.

➤ Serve with: Fruity rosé

Photo top: Linguine with Lemon Scampi   *Photo bottom:* Bucatini with Sardines ➤

Inexpensive |
Sophisticated
Tagliatelle with Crawfish

SERVES 4:

- ➤ 2 scallions
- 2 stalks celery
- 1 beefsteak tomato
- 1 pound tagliatelle (or fettucine)
- Salt
- 3 tbs butter
- ³/₄ cup fish stock
- Freshly ground pepper
- 8 oz crawfish tails

🕐 Prep time: 25 minutes
➤ Calories per serving: 590

1 | Rinse scallions, clean and chop finely. Rinse celery and dice very finely. Remove core from tomato, pour boiling water over it and peel. Cut tomato in half, remove seeds and dice.

2 | Cook pasta according to the basic recipe. Melt 1 tbs butter and briefly sauté celery and scallions. Add tomatoes and cook briefly. Pour in stock and reduce for 5 minutes.

3 | Season sauce to taste with salt and pepper. Add and heat crawfish tails. Stir in remaining butter to thicken sauce. Drain pasta briefly and transfer to plates. Pour sauce over the top.

➤ Serve with: Fruity, hearty white wine

Takes More Time
Squid-Ink Spaghetti with White Tomato Sauce

SERVES 4:

- ➤ 2¼ pounds firm, ripe tomatoes
- 3 sprigs basil
- 2 cloves garlic
- 1 onion
- 2 tbs olive oil
- 2 cups cream
- Salt
- Freshly ground pepper
- 1 pound squid-ink spaghetti
- 1½ oz salmon caviar

🕐 Prep time: 30 minutes
🕐 Draining time: 12 hours
➤ Calories per serving: 615

1 | Rinse tomatoes, remove stems and chop. Chop basil leaves and stems. Coarsely purée both ingredients using a blender or hand blender. Moisten a paper towel, squeeze out water and lay it in the bottom of a colander. Place colander on a pot. Pour in purée and drain for 12 hours.

2 | Peel garlic and onion, mince and sauté briefly in hot oil. Add juice that was drained and bring to a boil, skimming off any foam that forms. Reduce to about one fourth over high heat. Stir in cream and heat. Season with salt and pepper and keep warm.

3 | Cook pasta according to the basic recipe. Drain pasta. Mix tomato sauce with a hand blender until foamy, pour over pasta, sprinkle with caviar and serve immediately.

➤ Serve with: Smooth, round, full-bodied white wine

Pasta with Meat and Poultry

These nutritious pasta sauces are mainly found in northern Italy where even today, the pasta is served up with "Ragù Bolognese" on Sunday afternoons. The meat that was once finely chopped with a knife has long been replaced by pre-ground meat but a long stewing process still results in the same incomparable flavor. Luckily, there are also meat sauces that can be prepared quickly and easily.

Quick Recipes

Tagliatelle with Prosciutto Pepper Butter

SERVES 4:

➤ 1 pound tagliatelle (or fettucine) |
Salt | 4 oz sliced prosciutto |
3 oz butter | 1 tsp coarsely ground
pepper | 2 oz whole Parmesan

1 | Cook pasta according to the basic
recipe. In the meantime, cut prosciutto
into coarse strips. Melt butter and simply
warm prosciutto and pepper over low
heat, do not fry.

2 | Drain pasta briefly and toss with
prosciutto pepper butter. Season to taste
with salt. Transfer to plates and finely
shave Parmesan over the top using a
vegetable or cheese slicer.

Macaroni with Ground Beef Sauce

SERVES 4:

➤ 6 oz ground beef | 1 tbs soffritto
pronto (see page 10) | $^1/_4$ cup white
wine (may substitute vegetable stock) |
14 oz tomato sauce (see page 8) |
Salt | Freshly ground pepper |
1 pound macaroni | 2 oz freshly
grated Parmesan

1 | Sauté ground beef 4–5 minutes over
medium heat until it's slightly brown
and crumbly. Stir in soffritto and brown
briefly. Add wine and tomato sauce,
season with salt and pepper and stew for
20 minutes. Cook pasta according to the
basic recipe. Drain, transfer to plates and
top with sauce. Serve cheese on the side.

Easy | Spicy

Tagliolini all'Arrabbiata with Bacon

SERVES 4:

- 5 oz sliced bacon
- 1 onion
- 3 cloves garlic
- 2 red pepperoncini (or chile peppers)
- 1 pound tagliolini (or linguine)
- Salt
- 1 can chopped tomatoes (14 oz)
- 1 bunch basil
- Freshly ground pepper
- 3 oz freshly grated Pecorino

⏱ Prep time: 35 minutes

- Calories per serving: 760

1 | Cut bacon into very small cubes or narrow strips. Peel onion and garlic. Mince onion and chop garlic coarsely. Rinse pepperoncini, cut in half lengthwise, remove seeds, chop and purée along with garlic in a blender.

2 | Cook pasta according to the basic recipe. Sauté bacon over medium heat until translucent. Add onions and braise until golden.

3 | Stir in puréed pepperoncini and braise. Add tomatoes and gently simmer mixture uncovered for 15 minutes over low heat.

4 | Coarsely chop basil leaves. Season bacon sauce with salt and pepper. Drain pasta briefly and toss with sauce, basil and half the cheese. Transfer to plates and serve remaining cheese on the side.

- Serve with: Medium-bodied red wine

For Company | Fast

Tagliatelle alla Papalina

SERVES 4:

- 1 pound tagliatelle (or fettucine)
- Salt
- 2 tbs butter
- 6 oz frozen peas
- 2 cups cream
- 4 oz cooked ham (without fat or rind)
- 2 oz Gorgonzola
- Freshly ground pepper

⏱ Prep time: 20 minutes

- Calories per serving: 660

1 | Cook pasta according to the basic recipe. Melt butter and briefly cook peas over low heat. Pour in cream, bring to a boil and steep for about 7 minutes.

2 | Dice ham finely and stir into sauce along with Gorgonzola. Season with salt and pepper.

3 | Drain pasta briefly and transfer to plates. Top with sauce and serve.

- Serve with: Fruity sparkling wine

Specialty of Venice

Bucatini with Liver Pepper Sauce

SERVES 4:

➤ 9 oz chicken livers
2 anchovy fillets in brine
1 oz sliced bacon
1 small bunch parsley
2 cloves garlic
¾ cup white wine (may substitute vegetable stock)
1 tsp finely chopped lemon zest
1 tsp green peppercorns
1 pound bucatini
Salt
1 tbs lemon juice

🕑 Prep time: 30 minutes
➤ Calories per serving: 605

1 | Clean chicken livers and cut into small pieces. Rinse anchovy fillets and pat dry. Finely dice anchovies and bacon. Rinse parsley, shake dry and chop leaves very finely. Peel garlic.

2 | Fry bacon 1–2 minutes over medium heat until translucent, then add livers, anchovies and parsley and brown for 3 minutes.

3 | Squeeze garlic through a press and add. Pour in wine and stir in lemon zest and pepper. Gently simmer mixture uncovered for 10 minutes over low heat. Cook pasta according to the basic recipe.

4 | Season sauce to taste with salt and lemon juice. Drain pasta briefly, transfer to plates and top with sauce.

➤ Serve with: Fresh white wine with a hint of lemon

Easy | Hearty

Capellini with Leek and Sausage

SERVES 4:

➤ 9 oz leeks
2 tbs olive oil
12 oz raw bratwurst
4 oz crème fraîche
4 oz sour cream
Salt
Freshly ground pepper
Freshly grated nutmeg
12 oz capellini
2 oz freshly grated Grana Padano

🕑 Prep time: 30 minutes
➤ Calories per serving: 815

1 | Clean leak, cut open lengthwise, rinse thoroughly and cut into narrow strips. Heat oil and braise leek for about 5 minutes over low heat.

2 | Cut bratwurst into small pieces, squeeze the meat out of the skin and add the meat only to leek. Brown for 3 minutes while stirring. Stir together crème fraîche and sour cream, add to sausage and simmer for 5 minutes. Season to taste with salt, pepper and nutmeg.

3 | Cook pasta according to the basic recipe. Drain briefly and toss with the sauce. Serve cheese on the side.

➤ Serve with: Spicy white wine

Photo top: **Bucatini with Liver Pepper Sauce** *Photo bottom:* **Capellini with Leek and Sausage** ➤

For Gourmets
Reginette with Duck Breast

SERVES 4:

➤ 9 oz duck breast fillet
Salt
Freshly ground pepper
2 large zucchini
1 onion
1 tbs chopped parsley
1 cup white wine
(may substitute
vegetable stock)
1 pound reginette
1 tbs butter

🕐 Prep time: 45 minutes
➤ Calories per serving: 650

1 | Preheat oven to 250°F. Score skin on duck fillets in a diamond pattern and season with salt and pepper. Heat a non-stick pan and fry fillet over high heat for 5–6 minutes on each side, first on the skin side and then on the meat side. Remove from pan, cover and keep warm in the oven (center rack) until sauce is ready.

2 | Rinse and clean zucchini. Peel onion. Finely dice both ingredients and sauté in the pan in which the duck was cooked. Cook vegetables in duck fat for 5–7 minutes over medium heat until golden brown. Add parsley and cook briefly. Pour in wine and reduce by half uncovered over low heat.

3 | Cook pasta according to the basic recipe. Cut duck breast into thin slices, stir into sauce and season with salt and pepper. Drain pasta briefly and toss with butter. Transfer to plates and top with sauce.

➤ Serve with: Fruity, slightly chilled red wine

Fast | Sophisticated
Farfalle with Chicken Breast

SERVES 4:

➤ 9 oz chicken breast
(2–3 split breasts)
2 tbs butter
1 clove garlic
1/2 cup chicken stock
1 cup cream
Salt
Freshly ground pepper
1 pound farfalle
1 ball Mozzarella (4–5 oz)
3 sprigs basil

🕐 Prep time: 25 minutes
➤ Calories per serving: 615

1 | Cut chicken breasts into strips about 1/2 inch wide. Heat butter until foamy and sauté chicken strips for about 5 minutes over medium to high heat while stirring until lightly browned. Peel garlic, squeeze through a press and add. Pour in stock and cream. Season with salt and pepper and steep uncovered over low heat for 10 minutes.

2 | Cook pasta according to the basic recipe. Dice Mozzarella finely. Remove basil leaves from stems. Drain pasta and toss with sauce and Mozzarella. Serve sprinkled with basil.

➤ Serve with: Hearty, fruity white wine

Photo top: **Reginette with Duck Breast** *Photo bottom:* **Farfalle with Chicken Breast** ➤

Specialty of Tuscany | Takes More Time
Pappardelle with Rabbit Salmi

SERVES 4:

➤ 12 oz rabbit meat
(from saddle or leg,
skinned and deboned)

1 onion

1 carrot

1 stalk celery

1 sprig rosemary

1½ cups hearty red wine
(may substitute game
stock or vegetable stock)

2 tbs oil

4 tbs butter

Salt

Freshly ground pepper

1 pound pappardelle

A little flour for dredging

🕐 Prep time: 25 minutes
🕐 Marinating time: 12 hours
🕐 Cooking time: 50 minutes
➤ Calories per serving: 680

1 | Cut rabbit meat into bite-sized pieces. Peel and chop onion. Peel carrot, rinse and clean celery and dice both finely or cut into thin slices. Rinse rosemary sprig and shake dry. Place these prepared ingredients in a bowl with the wine, cover and marinate 12 hours in the refrigerator.

2 | Drain all ingredients in a colander, making sure you save the liquid. Pat meat dry with paper towels and dredge in flour seasoned with salt and pepper. Heat oil and half the butter and brown meat 4–6 minutes over high heat. Add marinated vegetables and brown 2–3 minutes.

Pour in half the marinade liquid and season with salt and pepper. Cover and stew for 45 min-utes over low heat, adding marinade if necessary.

3 | Thirty minutes into the stewing time, cook pasta according to the basic recipe. Drain briefly and toss with remaining butter. Season sauce to taste with salt and pepper and toss with pasta.

➤ Serve with: A not-too-heavy red wine

1 **Marinate**

Pour wine over prepared ingredients, cover and marinate, preferably overnight.

2 **Prepare Salmi**

Dredge rabbit in flour, brown and stew in the marinade along with marinated vegetables.

3 **Finish**

Cook pasta, season salmi to taste, toss together and serve immediately.

55

Easy | Hearty

Spaghetti with Meat Sauce

SERVES 4:

- 1 onion
  1 large carrot
  1 stalk celery
  1½ pounds tomatoes
  9 oz lean beef (not ground)
  3 tbs olive oil
  3 cloves garlic
  2 tbs tomato paste
  ⅔ cup red wine (may substitute vegetable stock)
  Salt
  Freshly ground pepper
  1 tsp oregano leaves
  1 tsp thyme leaves
  1 tsp rosemary needles
  1 pound spaghetti

- Prep time: 1 hour
- Calories per serving: 565

1 | Peel onion and carrot, rinse and clean celery and dice all three very finely. Remove cores from tomatoes, pour boiling water over them and peel. Cut tomatoes in half, remove seeds and dice.

2 | Cut meat into very small cubes. Heat oil and lightly brown meat for 7–10 minutes over medium heat. Peel garlic, squeeze through a press and add. Add onion, carrot and celery and cook for 5 minutes.

3 | Stir in tomato paste and wine and reduce almost completely. Then add tomatoes and stew uncovered for 10 minutes. Season with salt, pepper and herbs, cover and stew for 15–20 minutes. Cook pasta according to the basic recipe. Drain, transfer to plates and top with sauce.

Takes More Time

Matriciani with Lamb Ragù

SERVES 4:

- 9 oz lamb loin
  9 oz bell peppers
  1 onion
  2 cloves garlic
  3 tbs olive oil
  1 bay leaf
  ⅔ cup white wine (may substitute vegetable stock)
  14 oz tomatoes
  1 pound matriciani
  Salt
  Freshly ground pepper

- Prep time: 25 minutes
- Cooking time: 35 minutes
- Calories per serving: 550

1 | Cut lamb loin into bite-sized cubes. Rinse bell peppers, cut in half, clean and cut into diamonds. Peel onion and garlic and dice finely. Heat oil and brown bell pepper for 5 minutes over high heat, then remove from pan. Sauté onion and garlic in the same oil for 5 minutes over medium heat until translucent.

2 | Add lamb and bay leaf and brown for 5 minutes. Pour in wine and stew for 15 minutes uncovered over low heat. Remove cores from tomatoes, pour boiling water over them and peel. Cut in half, remove seeds and chop. Add tomatoes to meat and stew another 20 minutes.

3 | Cook pasta according to the basic recipe. Stir bell peppers into sauce and season to taste with salt and pepper. Drain pasta briefly and toss with the sauce.

Glossary

Arrabbiata

Literally "angry-woman style," this is a hearty, rustic tomato sauce from Abruzzo made spicy by red peperoncini. This fiery sauce is also very popular in Rome.

Bomba Vulcanica

"Bomba" means bomb, which is how this hot chili purée from Sicily and the Eolian Islands explodes on your tongue. It's made of red peperoncini, olive oil and spices and is used for seasoning pasta sauces or is spread on bruschetta (toasted bread slices).

Donna di Strada

Literally "street-walker style," this is a fruity sauce that can be quickly prepared from cherry tomatoes, a lot of garlic, anchovies, olives and capers. It is similar to the Neapolitan "Puttanesca" with peeled and chopped plum tomatoes.

Gremolata

Originally a mixture of chopped lemon zest, garlic and parsley that was then sprinkled on osso buco, gremolata is a versatile seasoning that has been transformed again and again and is now used for a variety of dishes.

Olio

In Italy, this always means olive oil, especially "extra virgin," i.e. cold-pressed and not chemically treated. Depending on the region it can have a mild, fruity or spicy flavor.

Panna

In Italy, "panna da cucina" is a thick cream used in sauces with a fat content of only 20%. You can substitute a mixture of equal parts crème fraîche and sour cream.

Papalina

Literally "skull-cap style," this specialty of Emilia-Romagna is easy to prepare. It is a cream sauce made of Gorgonzola, peas and cooked ham.

Parmigiana

This refers to a sauce or dish that was prepared using only butter and Parmesan.

Pepperoncini

Fresh or dried medium-length chili peppers about the width of a thumb that are mainly used in Abruzzo and southern Italy to season many sauces. They can range from hot to very hot. You may substitute either fresh or dried red chili peppers or cayenne pepper.

Pesto

Originally a purée of fresh basil, pine nuts, Pecorino and Parmesan which, in Liguria, is either thinned with a little pasta water to make a pasta sauce or is used to season vegetable soups. Traditionally, pesto is prepared using a marble mortar and boxwood pestle. Now it's mainly made in a blender. "Pesto rosso" from Veneto and Tuscany, on the other hand, is made of dried tomatoes and black olives and, like green pesto, is used in quick pasta sauces or spread on bruschetta (toasted bread slices).

Pinzimonio
Originally a sauce made from extra virgin olive oil, salt and coarsely chopped pepper that serves as a dip for raw vegetables in Tuscany. This sauce has now become a favorite throughout Italy and often serves as an accompaniment to pasta.

Pomodori
The Italian word for tomatoes. Peeled, canned tomatoes called "pelati," usually come from southern Italy and are always preferable to hot-house tomatoes for making sauces. Other useful types, both of which are canned, are "polpa di pomodoro," peeled and coarsely chopped tomatoes, and "passata," which are strained tomatoes.

Prosciutto
Salted, air-dried ham. The most famous types are Prosciutto di Parma and Prosciutto San Daniele. Both give sauces a delicate semi-spicy aroma. You may substitute bacon. Smoked

ham though, has an extremely strong flavor and would be too spicy for pasta sauces.

Ragù
A ragù is a pasta sauce made of large pieces of meat that must be gently stewed for many hours. The meat is often served separately, in which case only the spicy stewing stock is used for the pasta sauce.

Salmi
A stock made of wine, vegetables and herbs used for marinating dark meats. Meat and salmi are then cooked together to make a ragù.

Salsa
Can be translated literally as "sauce" but actually refers to a creamy pasta sauce with a butter base.

Soffritto
Base for sauces made of finely chopped onions, garlic, carrots, celery, mushrooms, herbs and sometimes a little bacon. All these ingredients are gently roasted before adding wine, stock and tomatoes.

Sugo
Means "sauce for pasta" and refers to a thick sauce containing vegetables, mushrooms, meat or fish and, most of all, tomatoes.

Tricolori
Means "three-colored," usually referring to the colors of the Italian flag—red, green and white.

Trifolati
Literally "truffle-flavored," although it usually refers to mushrooms prepared with olive oil, parsley and leek.

Vongole
Clams found in shallow sections of the Mediterranean and highly esteemed in Italy. You may also substitute fresh mussels.

ABBREVIATIONS
approx = approximately
oz = ounce
tsp = teaspoon
tbs = tablespoon

Using this Index

To help you find recipes containing specific ingredients more quickly, this index also lists various ingredients (such as salmon and tomatoes) in alphabetical order, followed by the corresponding recipes.

The Author

Over 30 years ago, Reinhardt Hess turned his hobby into a profession. He learned the trade at the largest German cooking magazine, then worked for cookbook publishers and for the past 10 years has been a freelance author. He has written or collaborated on over 40 cookbooks and wine guides, two of which were awarded the German Gastronomic Academy's silver medal. His favorite subjects are Italian cuisine and unusual, original recipes that he develops himself in his own kitchen.

The Photographer

Jörn Rynio works as a photographer in Hamburg, Germany. His customers include national and international magazines, book publishers and ad agencies. All the recipe photos in this book were produced in his studio with the energetic support of his food stylist, Martina Mehldau.

Photo Credits

FoodPhotographie Eising, Martina Görlach: cover photo
Teubner Foodfoto: S. 4, S. 6, S. 7, S. 9
All others: Jörn Rynio, Hamburg

Published originally under the title 1 Nudel—50 Saucen; Pasta für jeden Tag © 2002 Gräfe und Unzer Verlag GmbH, Munich. English translation for the U.S. market © 2002, Silverback Books, Inc.

Editors: Jonathan Silverman, Birgit Rademacker, Tanja Dusy
Translator: Christie Tam
Typesetting and DTP: Patty Holden, Redaktionsbüro Christina Kempe, Munich
Layout, typography and cover design: Independent Medien Design, Munich
Production: Helmut Giersberg
Reproduction: Repro Schmidt

Printed in Singapore

ISBN 978-1-930603-12-7

Enjoy Other Quick & Easy Books

1 Pan—50 Muffins

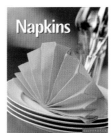

Napkins

Christmas Cookies

Fast Italian

Bargit Proebst

Sauces and Dips

Irresistible Fondue

Angelika Illies

Cooking for Two

Cornelia Adam

Healthy Wok

Elisabeth Doepp
Christian Willrich
Joerns Arnhold

Great flavorful and satisfying meals

Grilling

Antje Gruener

Chops, flavorful poultry—delectable morsels from the grill. Discover recipes, from spareribs to skewered vegetables, with sauces and chutneys.

Andreas Fürtmayr

Sushi

Classic ideas from Japan and new fusion sushi
Home-made perfectly.

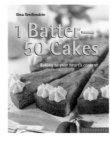

Gina Greifenstein

1 Batter—50 Cakes

Baking to your heart's content

Cooking in Clay

Healthy Recipes with Great Flavor

Erika Casparek-Türkkan

1 Noodle, 50 Sauces

Everyday Pasta • Old and New Italian Dishes
Noodle biography • 10 Tips for Success

Chris Muliar

Cocktails for Drivers

100% Enjoyment

Antipasti and Tapas

Mediterranean Appetizers
Cornelia Schinharl

Soups

Classic to Contemporary

Sebastian Dickhaut

Claudia Schmidt

Raclette

New Recipes with Cheese Primer and Party Dips

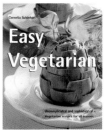

Cornelia Schinharl

Easy Vegetarian

Uncomplicated and sophisticated •
Vegetarian recipes for all seasons

Cornelia Adam

Garlic

Marlisa Szwillus

Fondue

Cheese, vegetable, broth kinds
of meat—discover them all right at
the table. Good than techniques.

Sebastian Dickhaut

Casseroles

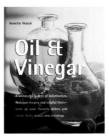

Annette Heisch

Oil & Vinegar

A wonderful source of information,
delicious recipes and helpful hints—
liven up your favorite dishes and
create tasty sauces and dressings.

Cornelia Adam

Quiche

Delicious, savory pies with
vegetables, meat, poultry, or
fish—ones for all seasons

PASTA

- Pasta made from pure, durum wheat can be cooked al dente and is best for accenting the sauce.
- Good pasta is not cheap; less expensive types are often sticky and doughy.
- Check the expiration date; old pasta tastes slightly moldy.

Guaranteed Success for Pasta and Sauces

SAUCES

- Sauces should be thick enough to coat the pasta but not glue it together.
- Quick sauces should be lightly spiced; sauces stewed over a long period of time can be more heavily seasoned.
- A small bit of butter or olive oil added at the end gives the sauce extra flavor.

HERBS

- For quick, light sauces, use fresh herbs, e.g. basil, flat-leaved parsley, oregano or marjoram.
- For stewed sauces, you can also use dried herbs, which traditionally include bay leaves, thyme, oregano, sage and rosemary.

CHEESE

- Pre-grated cheese in a plastic bag spoils the best sauce.
- Buy whole chunks of Parmigiano Reggiano, Grana Padano and Pecorino and grate them fresh.
- Wrap leftover cheese in paper towels soaked with vinegar and store in the vegetable bin.